DATE DUE

AWESOME VALUES IN FAMOUS LIVES

Jimmy Carter

A Life of Service

Barbara Kramer

Enslow Elementary
an imprint of

Enslow Publishers, Inc.

40 Industrial Road	PO Box 38
Box 398	Aldershot
Berkeley Heights, NJ 07922	Hants GU12 6BP
USA	UK

http://www.enslow.com

Enslow Elementary, an imprint of Enslow Publishers, Inc.

Enslow Elementary® is a registered trademark of Enslow Publishers, Inc.

Library of Congress Cataloging-in-Publication Data

Kramer, Barbara.
    Jimmy Carter : a life of service / Barbara Kramer.
        p. cm. — (Awesome values in famous lives)
    Includes bibliographical references and index.
    ISBN 0-7660-2379-6
    1. Carter, Jimmy, 1924–   . —Juvenile literature. 2. Carter, Jimmy, 1924– . Contributions in social
service—Juvenile literature. 3. Presidents—United States—Biography—Juvenile literature. 4. Social values—
United States—Case studies—Juvenile literature. 5. Social service—United States—Case studies—Juvenile
literature. I. Title. II. Series.
E873.K73 2005
973.926'092—dc22

                                                                                          2004004506

Printed in the United States of America

10 9 8 7 6 5 4 3 2 1

To Our Readers: We have done our best to make sure all Internet Addresses in this book were active and appropriate when we went to press. However, the author and the publisher have no control over and assume no liability for the material available on those Internet sites or on other Web sites they may link to. Any comments or suggestions can be sent by e-mail to comments@enslow.com or to the address on the back cover.

Every effort has been made to locate all copyright holders of material used in this book. If any errors or omissions have occurred, corrections will be made in future editions of this book.

Illustration Credits: AP/WideWorld, pp. 4, 6, 8, 24, 37, 42, 43B; Jerry Battle <http://www.jerry battle.com>, pp. 7, 17, 43T; Enslow Publishers, Inc., p. 28; Hemera Technologies, Inc., p. 31; Courtesy of the Jimmy Carter Library, pp. 2, 10, 12, 13, 14, 15, 16, 19, 22, 23, 27, 29, 30, 32–33, 35, 40, 46; A Poyo, courtesy of the Jimmy Carter Library, p. 39; Library of Congress, p. 9, 20; The Carter Center, p. 38.

Cover Illustration: Jimmy Carter Library.

Contents

1. A Small-Town Boy 5

2. A Change of Plans 11

3. "I'm Jimmy Carter" 18

4. Mr. President 25

5. "A Man of Peace" 34

Timeline 43

Words to Know 44

Chapter Notes 45

Learn More About Jimmy Carter 46

Internet Addresses 47

Index 48

CHAPTER 1

A Small-Town Boy

The ringing of the telephone woke Jimmy Carter from a deep, nighttime sleep. Who was calling at 4:02 A.M.? Was something wrong? Jimmy's wife picked up the phone, then shouted, "Jimmy! Jimmy!"[1] The call came from far away in Oslo, Norway, where it was already 10:02 A.M. The caller had some exciting news: Jimmy Carter had won the Nobel Peace Prize for 2002.

The Nobel Peace Prize is one of the world's highest honors. It was being awarded to Jimmy Carter to honor all that he had done for peace. Jimmy had worked for peace as the thirty-ninth president of the United States. A few years later, he founded the Carter Center to work for peace, better health, and fairness for all the people of the world.

James Earl Carter, Jr., was born in Plains on October 1, 1924. Most people called him Jimmy. When Jimmy was four, his family moved to a farm a few miles away, near Archery, Georgia. Jimmy's father was a farmer. He also ran a small store in Archery that sold farm supplies.

Jimmy's mother taught him to be kind and fair to everyone.

When Jimmy was a child, his house had no heat,
no running water, and no electric lights.

There was always work to do on the Carter farm,
and everyone helped. Jimmy was only five years old
when he started his own business selling boiled
peanuts. He picked peanuts in his father's field. He
washed them and soaked them overnight in salty
water. In the morning he boiled them. After the
peanuts cooled, he put them into paper bags and

Jimmy was the eldest of four children. In this photo, Jimmy was six years old, and his sister Gloria was four.

walked three miles to Plains. There, he sold his boiled peanuts for a nickel a bag.

Jimmy also did chores on the farm. He hauled buckets of drinking water to the workers in the fields. He gathered eggs and fed the chickens. As he grew bigger and stronger, the work got harder. Jimmy picked cotton and peanuts by hand. He plowed the fields with a plow pulled by a mule. He learned to fix farm machines and helped out in his father's store.

Jimmy worked hard, but there was also time for fun. He and his friends flew kites and built treehouses. They went swimming, rode horses, and explored the woods. Jimmy liked hunting and fishing, too.

Jimmy's friends were the children of the African-American field hands on his father's farm. Jimmy and his friends worked side by side and played together. But they could not go to the same schools or churches. Laws in those days kept black people and white people apart. This is called segregation. Jimmy went to a school for white children. His friends went to the school for black children.

Blacks and whites could not even drink from the same water fountain.

Like most of his friends and neighbors in Plains, Jimmy's father agreed with the segregation laws. His mother, Lillian, had a different view. She paid no attention to the color of people's skin.

Lillian was a nurse who took care of sick people in their homes. Some of her patients were white, and others were black. She treated everyone the same. From his mother, Jimmy learned that all people are equal. "My mother's quiet service to others . . . was a good lesson for me," he wrote.[2]

Jimmy played tennis and was on the school basketball team. He read anytime he got a chance. "Mama and I always had a magazine or book to read while eating our meals," he said.[3] He earned A's in all his classes at Plains High School. Doing well in school was important to Jimmy. He had big plans for his life.

CHAPTER 2

A Change of Plans

Jimmy dreamed of being a sailor when he grew up. "I want to go to Annapolis and be a Naval officer," he said.[1] Jimmy planned to attend the U.S. Naval Academy in Annapolis, Maryland.

Jimmy graduated from high school in 1941. To prepare for the naval academy, he first had to take some college courses in math and science.

Then, in 1943, Jimmy began his studies for the navy. One day, on a visit home to Plains, Jimmy went on a date with his sister's best friend, Rosalynn Smith. They saw a movie together. When he got home, Jimmy told his mother, "She's the girl I want to marry."[2]

Jimmy graduated from the naval academy in June 1946. In July, he and Rosalynn were married. They moved to Norfolk, Virginia, where Jimmy worked on a battleship, the USS *Wyoming*.

Jimmy had wanted to be in the navy since he was five years old.

Rosalynn, left, and Jimmy's mother pinned the shoulder bars on his uniform in June 1946.

Two years later, Jimmy took the navy's class to learn about submarines. In Pearl Harbor, Hawaii, he became an officer on a submarine, the USS *Pomfret*.

While Jimmy was in the navy, he kept on studying and learning. He worked on ships in California, Connecticut, and New York. During those years, the Carters had three sons, John William (called Jack); James Earl III (Chip); and Donnel Jeffrey (Jeff).

Jimmy and
Rosalynn were
married on
July 7, 1946.

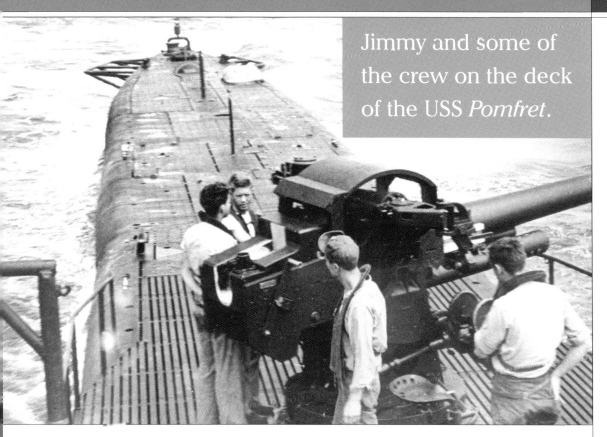

Jimmy and some of the crew on the deck of the USS *Pomfret*.

In 1953, Jimmy went back to Plains, Georgia, to see his father, who was dying. Jimmy was amazed at how many people came to visit his father and say good-bye. His father was a leader in the church and in the community. He taught Sunday school and was a member of the school board, the group that ran the public schools. He had been elected to the Georgia State Legislature, which is the part of the government that made the laws.

At his father's bedside, Jimmy heard stories about how his father had helped people in small ways, too—lending them money or buying clothes. At his father's funeral, people filled the church to honor him. Jimmy began to think about his own life. What was he doing to help others?

Jimmy had been in the navy for many years. He had the life he had dreamed of since he was a little boy. After his visit home, Jimmy changed his mind. He decided to leave the navy and

Rosalynn with sons Jack, Jeff, and Chip.

Jimmy moved back to his family's peanut farm.

move his family back to Plains, Georgia. He wanted to
help his mother run the family farm and peanut
business. Most of all, Jimmy wanted to serve his
community the way his father had done.[3]

CHAPTER 3

"I'm Jimmy Carter"

J immy's first year back in Plains was a hard one. No rain fell for a long time, and the crops dried up in the fields. The Carter farm did not make much money that year. Luckily, the next season was better.

While Jimmy farmed and ran his peanut business in Plains, important changes were taking place in the country. In 1954, the

Jimmy's father had built a peanut warehouse. Peanuts from other farms in the area were kept in the warehouse, too.

Supreme Court—the highest court in the United States—ruled against school segregation. Jimmy was glad, but many white people in the South were angry. They did not want their children in the same classrooms as African-American children.

At last, the laws were changing. Jimmy had always hated segregation.

The News

HIGH COURT BANS
SEGREGAT   IN
BLIC

A group called the White Citizens' Council formed to keep schools segregated. Joining the group cost $5. All the white men in Plains were eager to be part of the council—except Jimmy. "I've got $5," he told them, "and I'd flush it down the toilet before I'd give it to you."[1] The other men were so angry that for a while they did not talk to Jimmy. But no one could change his belief that all people are equal.

Even though Jimmy had different ideas, he was an important person in Plains. He taught Sunday school and joined the groups running the hospital, the library, and the public schools.

In 1962 he was voted into the Georgia State Senate, where he worked for better education and civil rights. Two years later, Jimmy was elected to another term as senator. In 1966, he wanted to be governor of Georgia, but did not get enough votes. "It was the first real defeat in my life," he said.[2]

The Carters' daughter, Amy, was born in 1967. By then, Jimmy was making plans to run again

Jimmy worked hard to win votes.

for governor. This time he won. When he took office in January 1971, Jimmy spoke out about being fair to all people. "The time for racial discrimination is over," he said.[3] As governor, Jimmy hired African Americans for many state jobs. He hung a portrait of Martin Luther King, Jr., in the state capitol. It was the first time an African American had been honored in that way.

Jimmy also worked for better health care, schools, and state prisons. He found ways to save money in running the state government.

One day, Jimmy's mother asked what he planned to do when his term as governor ended in 1974. "I'm going to run for President," he said.[4] Jimmy's mother thought he was joking. "President of what?" she teased.[5] But Jimmy was serious.

How could a peanut farmer from Georgia become president of the United States? Most Americans had never even heard of him. In 1975, Jimmy traveled across the country to meet people everywhere. "I'm Jimmy Carter, and I'm going to be your next President," he said.[6]

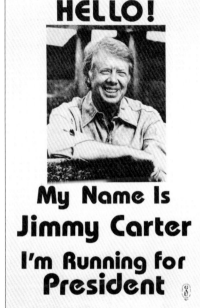

HELLO!

My Name Is Jimmy Carter I'm Running for President

Soon people all over the United States were talking about Jimmy Carter. To win the election, he would have to beat President Gerald R. Ford. Would people vote for Ford or for Carter? In November 1976, Jimmy Carter won the election.

Jimmy thanked the voters who elected him president, with Rosalynn and Amy at his side.

CHAPTER 4

Mr. President

On January 20, 1977, Jimmy Carter was sworn in as president of the United States. The ceremony took place on the steps of the U.S. Capitol in Washington, D.C. Then President Carter and his family began the drive down Pennsylvania Avenue to the White House. Thousands of people lined the street to get a look at the new president and first lady.

The Carters had not gone far when Jimmy told the driver to stop. "Let's go!" he said to his family. They stepped out of the car and began walking.[1]

At first, many people were shocked. They could not believe the president had left the safety of his bulletproof car. Then the crowd began to cheer. For Jimmy, it was a very special moment. "It was bitterly cold, but we felt warm inside," he said.[2]

Save Energy!

Laws passed when Carter was president are still helping Americans save energy. Builders must make homes that can be heated and cooled with less energy. Today's cars must be designed to use less gas.

President Carter cared about the environment. He created the Department of Energy and asked Americans to save energy, too. One way to do that was to turn down the heat in their homes. Keeping their homes a little cooler meant using less energy. At the White House, the Carters did the same.

By walking, Carter showed Americans that he was a regular person, just like everyone else.

Carter also created the Department of Education. New laws were passed to help students borrow money to pay for college. There were many programs to make schools better.

A high point for President Carter took place at Camp David in the mountains of Maryland. At

Camp David, the United States president and his family can get away from the hustle and bustle of Washington, D.C. It is also a good place for the president to hold important meetings. In September 1978, Carter met there with President Sadat of Egypt and the leader of Israel, Prime Minister Begin.

For many years, Israel had been at war with Arab countries, including Egypt, in the Middle East. Carter believed that the United States needed to be a leader for world peace. As a first step, he wanted to help Egypt and Israel make a peace treaty.

It was not an easy job. It seemed as if Sadat and Begin could not agree on anything. For a while, they were so angry that they refused to be in the same room. President Carter was patient. He met with them one at a time. Then he took messages back and forth between them. After thirteen days

It was a great moment in history when Prime Minister Begin, far left, shook hands with President Sadat, right.

Amy was nine years old when she moved into the White House with her parents.

of talks, they finally came to an agreement, and it led to a peace treaty between the two countries.

The lowest point in Carter's term as president came on November 4, 1979. Angry students broke into the American Embassy in the country of Iran.

They took sixty-six Americans hostage. The students later released some of the Americans, but fifty-three were not let go.

Carter talked to the government of Iran. He tried to find a peaceful way to bring the Americans home. When that did not work, he took a risk. In April 1980, he sent United States soldiers on a secret mission to free the hostages. The rescue mission did not succeed.

Carter ran for re-election in 1980. This time, he did not travel all over the country to meet people and win votes. He wanted to give his full attention to freeing the American hostages.

Tie a Yellow Ribbon

In the United States, Americans tied yellow ribbons around trees as a way to show that they cared about the hostages held in Iran. The yellow ribbons were a sign of freedom. Since then, Americans have used yellow ribbons to show they are thinking about all the soldiers who are fighting for freedom around the world.

Carter lost the election, but he used his last two months as president to keep on working for the release of the hostages.

On January 21, 1981, Ronald Reagan was sworn into office as the new president. A few minutes later, Carter and the nation got good news. After more than a year, the hostages were finally set free.

The Carter family at the White House in 1980. Standing, from left: Annette; Jeff; Chip; Rosalynn's mother, Allie M. Smith; the president; Amy, holding Jason's hand; Rosalynn; Jack and Judy, holding Sarah. Seated, from left: grandson James and Jimmy's mother, Lillian.

CHAPTER 5

"A Man of Peace"

W hen Carter's term as president ended, he went home to Plains, Georgia. What would he do with the rest of his life? Before he could answer that question, Carter had business problems to handle. While he was in the White House, Carter had put other people in charge of his farm and peanut business. He returned to find that the business was not doing well, and he had to sell it.

Other jobs kept him busy, too. He decided to write a book about his years as president. Much of the information for the book was in his diaries. He began reading and sorting through more than six thousand pages of notes in his diary.

Another job was raising money and making plans for his presidential library. The library would hold all the papers and other records of his life and his time in the White House.

How would Carter spend his time after the presidency?

Carter also became a visiting professor at Emory University in Atlanta, Georgia. There, he talks to classes of college students about history, politics, law, and world affairs.

Homes for Everyone

In 1984, Carter began volunteering for Habitat for Humanity. For one week each year, he helps build homes for people who can not afford to buy one. Carter got a great deal of attention for that work. "People think that's all I do," he said.[1] But Carter does much more. By the 1990s, he was becoming better known for his work at the Carter Center.

Carter's days were busy, but he wanted to do something more important with his time.[2] He had spent more than half his life in public service. He wanted to keep doing work that would help other people.

He soon had his answer. "I want to provide a place where conflicts around the world can be solved," he said.[3] In 1982, in partnership with Emory University, he founded the Carter Center to work for peace and better health all over the world.

Through the Carter Center, Jimmy has worked as a peacemaker in countries such as Haiti, North Korea, Sudan, Liberia, and Venezuela. Leaders invite him to their countries to help settle arguments. He listens to both sides and then tries to help people reach an agreement.

The Carter Center watches over voting and elections around the world. Carter and others have traveled to countries such as Panama, Nicaragua, and Mexico to make sure their elections are fair.

Years earlier, Jimmy had built furniture for his first house. Now he was putting his skills to use to help Habitat for Humanity.

These children welcomed Jimmy to Ghana in Africa.

The Carter Center also has farming and health programs to help people in some of the world's poorest countries.

When Jimmy Carter won the Nobel Peace Prize in 2002, it came with a one-million-dollar award. He gave the money to the Carter Center. He knows the center will never stop working for peace and health around the world.

Many people believe that Carter has done his best work in the years since he left the White House. Carter says that now he has the freedom to choose the projects he wants to do. "As President, I wouldn't have had time to do all the things I'm doing now," he said.[4]

When he is not traveling the world as part of his work for the Carter Center, Jimmy Carter

Carter wore African clothing in Ghana and was named an honorary village chief. He was there to help fight disease in Africa.

Carter has traveled to many countries to work for peace.
Here, he met with North Korean president Kim Il Sung.

lives an ordinary life in Georgia. He rides his bicycle through the streets of Plains and takes his turn mowing the church lawn. He goes fishing, plays tennis, and walks or jogs. He also teaches a Sunday school class. Many of the people who attend his classes are visitors from all around the world and from all different religions. One Sunday, his class had guests from twenty-eight different countries.

Jimmy Carter, Author

Carter is the author of nineteen books. He has written about politics, history, and his life. He wrote a book of poetry and a children's book that his daughter, Amy, illustrated. In 2003 his first novel, *The Hornet's Nest: A Novel of the Revolutionary War*, was published.

A reporter once asked Carter how he wanted to be remembered. "As a man of peace," he said, "and a good husband and father."[5] Carter is known all over the world as a peacemaker. He has devoted his life to his family and to serving others. He has never stopped working for a better community, country, and world.

Carter has won many awards and honors
for his life of service to others. Here, he holds
the Lions Humanitarian Award.

Timeline

1924   Born in Plains, Georgia, on October 1.

1928   Family moves to a farm near the community of Archery.

1941   Graduates from Plains High School.

1946   Graduates from the U.S. Naval Academy. Marries Rosalynn Smith.

1962   Is elected to the Georgia State Senate.

1970   Is elected governor of Georgia.

1977   Takes office as the thirty-ninth president of the United States.

1980   Loses the election for another term as president.

1982   Starts the Carter Center to work for peace and health worldwide.

1986   Opens the Jimmy Carter Library and Museum.

2002   Accepts the Nobel Peace Prize.

Words to Know

American Embassy—The home or office for United States government workers in a foreign country.

candidate—A person who is running for an office such as governor or president.

capitol—The building where lawmakers meet.

civil rights—The rights of all people in a country no matter what their religion, skin color, or other differences.

conflict—A disagreement or a fight.

defeat—To lose a contest or election.

Democratic Party—One of the two main groups that wants its members to run the government of the United States. The other group is called the Republican Party.

hostage—A person who is held prisoner by another person or a group until demands are met.

racial discrimination—Treating people unfairly because of the color of their skin.

treaty—An agreement between countries.

U.S. Naval Academy—The school that trains people to be officers in the U.S. Navy.

Chapter Notes

CHAPTER 1.
A Small-Town Boy

1. "Jimmy Carter: Peace Seeker," *People*, December 30, 2002, p. 92.

2. Jimmy Carter, *Talking Peace: A Vision for the Next Generation* (New York: Dutton Children's Books, 1995, revised edition), p. 24.

3. Jimmy Carter, *An Hour Before Daylight: Memories of a Rural Boyhood* (New York: Simon & Schuster, 2001), p. 32.

CHAPTER 2.
A Change of Plans

1. Robert Epstein, Ph.D., "The Making of a Peacemaker," *Psychology Today*, January/February 2002, p. 73.

2. Jimmy Carter, *Why Not the Best?* (Nashville: Broadman Press, 1975), p. 72.

3. *Why Not the Best?*, p. 69.

CHAPTER 3.
"I'm Jimmy Carter"

1. Patrick Anderson, "Peanut Farmer for President," *New York Times Magazine*, December 14, 1975, p. 71.

2. "Interview: James E. Carter Jr.," © 2004 Academy of Achievement, <http://www.achievement.org/autodoc/page/car0int-1> (September 22, 2004).

3. "New Day A'Coming in the South," *Time*, May 31, 1971, p. 14.

4. "I'm Jimmy Carter, and . . . ," *Time*, January 3, 1977, p. 14.

5. "I'm Jimmy Carter" article.

6. "I'm Jimmy Carter" article, p. 11.

CHAPTER 4.
Mr. President

1. Jimmy Carter, *Keeping Faith: Memoirs of a President* (New York: Bantam Books, 1982), p. 17.

2. *Keeping Faith*, p. 17.

CHAPTER 5.
"A Man of Peace"

1. Jim Wooten, "The Conciliator," *New York Times Magazine*, January 29, 1995, p. 33.

2. Eleanor Clift, "A Man with a Mission," *Newsweek*, October 3, 1994, p. 36.

3. "A Man with a Mission" article, p. 36.

4. Stanley W. Cloud, "Hail to the Ex-Chief," *Time*, September 11, 1989, p. 60.

5. Brigette Lacombe, "Jimmy Carter: Peace Seeker," *People*, December 30, 2002, p. 92.

Learn More

George, Linda and Charles. *Jimmy Carter: Builder of Peace.* Chicago: Children's Press, 2000.

Joseph, Paul. *Jimmy Carter.* Edina, Minn.: ABDO Publishing Company, 2002.

Margaret, Amy. *Jimmy Carter Library and Museum.* New York: PowerKids Press, 2004.

Santella, Andrew. *James Earl Carter, Jr.* Minneapolis: CompassPoint Books, 2002.

Internet Addresses

The Kids Page has a variety of information including a short biography, photos, fun facts, and a timeline showing events that took place when Jimmy was a boy.

<http://www.jimmycarterlibrary.org>

Features a short biography about Jimmy Carter. Clicking on "Kid Bios" leads to a biography about him written by a student.

<http://www.whitehouse.gov/history/presidents>

The Jimmy Carter National Historical Site Education Program includes virtual tours of Jimmy's boyhood home, the farm, and Plains High School. A "Games & Fun" page has word searches, a secret code to solve, and recipes for making items such as peanut butter and peanut butter playdough.

<http://www.sowega.net/~plainsed>

Index

A

African Americans, 9, 19, 22
American Embassy in Iran, 30
    hostage crisis, 31, 33
Annapolis, Maryland, 11
Archery, Georgia, 6

B

Begin, Menachem, 28, **29**

C

Camp David, **28**
Carter Center, 6, 36, 37, 38–39
Carter, Amy (daughter), 22, **24**, **27**, **30**, **32**
Carter, Chip (son), 13, **16**, **32**
Carter, Gloria (sister), **8**
Carter, Jack (son), 13, **16**, **33**
Carter, James Earl, Sr. (father), 6, 10, 15–16
Carter, Jeff (son), 13, **16**, **32**
Carter, Jimmy, **10**, **35**
    against segregation, 10, 21, 22
    as president, 6, 25, 26, **27**, **28**–31, **29**, **30**, **32**, 33
    as senator and governor, 21, **22**
    awards, **4**, 5, 6, 38, **42**
    books, 35, 41
    childhood, **6**, **7–8**, 9
    education, 10, 11, 12
    in the navy, **12**, **13**, **15**
    life after presidency, 34–35, 36, 41
    marriage, 12, **14**
    runs family farm, 16–17, 18–**19**
    runs for president, 23, **24**
    work for peace, 6, 36, **37**, 38–**39**, **40**, 41
Carter, Lillian (mother), **6**, 10, **13**, **33**
Carter, Rosalyn (wife), 5, 12, **13**, **14**, **16**, **24**, **27**, **32**, 37

D

Department of Education, 28
Department of Energy, 26

E

Egypt, 28, 29
Emory University, 36

F

Ford, Gerald R., 23

G

Georgia State Senate, 21
Ghana, Africa, **38**, **39**

H

Habitat for Humanity, 36, **37**

I

Iran, 31
Israel, 28, 29

K

Kim Il Sung, **40**
King, Martin Luther, Jr., 22

N

Nobel Peace Prize, **5**, 6, 38
Norfolk, Virginia, 12
North Korea, 37, **40**

O

Oslo, Norway, 5

P

Pearl Harbor, Hawaii, 13
Plains High School, 10
Plains, Georgia, 6, 12, 15, **17**, 18, 21, 34
presidential library, 35

R

Regan, Ronald, 33

S

Sadat, Anwar, 28, **29**
segregation, **9**
    banned in schools, 19, **20**
Smith, Rosalyn. *See* Carter, Rosalyn

U

U.S. Naval Academy, 11
USS *Pomfret*, 13, **15**
USS *Wyoming*, 12

W

Washington, D.C., 25, **28**
White Citizens' Council, 21
White House, 26, **30**, **32–33**